# Picking
# "Growth" Stocks

by T. Rowe Price, Jr.

▼

BARRON'S
*The National Financial Weekly*
NEW YORK

The contents of this booklet represents a reprint
of a series of articles which was published in
BARRON'S in May-June, 1939.

# Foreword

ABOUT 15 years ago an investment philosophy was developed which became very popular in the pre-depression days. This philosophy was based on the premise that American industry had a long period of substantial growth ahead of it. As a result, the argument ran, the conservative investor could safely share in the industrial growth of his country by holding common stocks—specifically, the shares of leading corporations.

For a while this theory appeared to work, but those who followed it and held their common stocks, bought in the 1929 boom, straight through the following decade have found that considerable variation now exists among different corporations as respects the rate of their growth. Some have actually retrogressed.

To investors with a long-range point of view, the selection of securities in growing industries and companies is extremely important, but the difficulties of achieving such a selection have become increasingly great as the growth of industry in general has slowed down.

The author of this study began to work out a theory of investment, based on a recognition of the fact that corporations have life cycles similar to those of humans, nearly 10 years ago. Since 1934 he has tested the soundness of his theory by applying it to an actual fund. The results of this investment experience are strong evidence that the restriction of one's investments to "growth" stocks is sound in practice as well as in theory.

## Chapter I

# Corporations, Like People, Have Life Cycles - Risks Increase When Maturity Is Reached

IN planning an investment program, it is extremely important that the investor, before purchasing any securities, should ask himself, "What is my objective?" He must realize that except over a long period of years no common stock investment can give him safety of capital and that there may be other mediums more likely to provide him with a liberal, steady income.

## Conserving Assets, Income or Market Appreciation

The three major objectives of investors are: (1) *Capital conservation*, or stability of market value of invested principal; (2)*Liberal income* at a fixed rate; and (3) *Capital growth*. While all securities involve risk, the degree varies widely in accordance with the type of security. One type, such as short-term government bonds, might well serve as a medium for safety of principal, but certainly should not be expected to produce substantial profits.

Another type, such as the common stock of an aviation company, might produce substantial profits, but certainly should not be expected to provide safety of principal. Either security may be qualified to do one job well, but no one security possesses the qualifications to accomplish all three major objectives. The individual must, therefore, determine in advance what percentage of his total fund should be invested for capital conservation, how much for liberal income and how much for capital growth, and then select the type of security best qualified to accomplish each objective.

By way of illustration, Chart I is presented to show the results which were realized during the year 1938 from each portion of a diversified fund. The extreme fluctuations in security values which were witnessed during 1938 afford a fair test of the value of such a policy.

CHART I

Value and Income in 1938 on Diversified Investment Fund

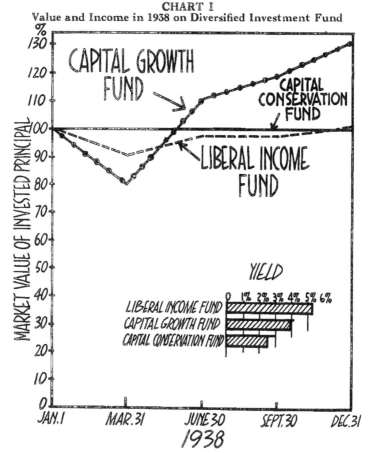

The capital conservation portion of the fund, which amounted to 20% of the whole and had as its primary objective stability of market value, fluctuated a maximum of only ½ of 1% between 100 at the beginning of the period and 100.5 at the end, but the income was only 2.58% and profit possibilities were negligible. This portion of the fund consisted of highest grade short-term bonds and bank deposits.

The liberal income portion of the fund, which had as its primary objective relatively high income at a fixed rate, yielded 5.33%, but the fund fluctuated in market value from 100 at the beginning of the year to 90.5 on March 31, and back to 100.9 on December 31. Profit possibilities were limited. Bonds below the topmost grade and preferred stocks made up this 30% of the total fund.

### Common Stocks for Capital Growth

The capital growth portion of the fund, described in detail in a subsequent chapter increased 31%, but lacked stability in market value, having declined 20% from the first of the year to March 31. Income of 4.03%, while reasonably high, was lower than the return on the liberal income portion of the fund. This half of the total fund, designed for capital growth, consisted entirely of common stocks.

To summarize, the chart illustrates that when money is invested for capital conservation, both liberal income and opportunity for capital growth are sacrificed; when money is invested for liberal income at a fixed rate, both stability of market value and capital growth are sacrificed; and when money is invested for capital growth, the other two major objectives, capital conservation and liberal income, must be sacrificed.

The "life cycle theory of investing", which is the main subject of this study, is equally applicable to the purchase of securities for capital conservation and liberal income as it is to the selection of securities for capital growth. In the explanation which follows, however, the discussion has been concentrated on common stocks because, as a class, they usually involve greater risks than bonds and preferred stocks, and because they are more sensitive to changing business trends. The "life cycle theory of investing", as applied to common stocks alone, does not constitute a complete investment program, since it does not guarantee either safety of capital or the highest, steady income. So far as that portion of an investor's funds designed to achieve capital growth is concerned, it does, in the author's opinion, afford the maximum gain with the minimum risk.

7

### Three Phases of the Corporate Life Cycle

Earnings of most corporations pass through a life cycle which, like the human life cycle, has three important phases—growth, maturity and decadence. Insurance companies know that a greater risk is involved in insuring the life of a man 50 years old than of a man 25, and that a much greater risk is involved in insuring a man of 75 than one of 50. They know, in other words, that risk increases as a man reaches maturity and starts to decline.

In very much the same way, common sense tells us that an investment in a business affords greater gain possibilities and involves less risk of loss while the long-term, or secular, earnings trend is still growing than after it has reached maturity and starts to decline. Once a business is well established, the greatest opportunity for gain is afforded during the period of growth in earning power. The risk factor increases when maturity is reached and decadence begins.

So much is fairly obvious. As long as American industry in general was in the growing phase, investors could choose almost blindly without great danger, although, of course, even then there were companies or industries which had already passed out of the growth phase. Now, however, the situation has changed. American industry in large part appears to have reached the phase of maturity, and careful search is necessary to determine the companies whose earnings are still in the growth phase and which, therefore, afford the maximum gain with the minimum risk of loss.

Because the economic or business cycle runs concurrently with a company's life cycle, it is difficult to determine in advance when earning power is on the decline. Research and an understanding of social, political and economic trends, however, should enable one to recognize the change in the long-term earnings trend of a business in time to withdraw his capital before it is seriously impaired.

### A Fully Invested Fund, 1935-38

The best proof that it *is* possible to select the stocks of companies which are in the growth phase is the experience of an actual fund to which has been applied what the author calls "the life cycle theory of investing". This theory has been developed over a period of approximately 10 years. In 1934 a small experimental fund was created in order to test the soundness of the theory. Since that time the principles and methods which are described in this and the following chapters have been used in the management of this actual fund, with the following results:

Throughout the four year period 1935-38 the fund has been fully invested—no attempt was made, in other words, to catch the swings of the market. Frequent changes were made, however, in the list of growth stocks. Radical legislation and sudden and far-reaching economic developments during the period have altered the long-term earnings trends of many corporations. When stocks appeared to have reached their maximum earning power they were liquidated and the proceeds reinvested in other growth stocks. Naturally, not every selection was a successful one.

The increase in principal of this experimental fund from Dec. 31, 1934, to Dec. 31, 1938, amounted to 76.3%. During that time the gain in the *Dow-Jones* composite average, which is made up of industrials, rails and utilities, was only 31.6%. The *Dow-Jones* average of 30 industrial stocks appreciated 48.7% during these four years. Chart II (see page 10) shows the progress of principal and income of the growth stock fund compared with the composite average.

Growth of income on the experimental fund is also impressive when compared with that of the *Dow-Jones* averages. Income on the fund and averages is shown in the following table for each of the four years, the return being expressed as a percentage of the original principal.

|  | 1935 | 1936 | 1937 | 1938 | 4 yr. avge. |
|---|---|---|---|---|---|
| Growth stock portfolio | 2.6% | 7.8% | 9.0% | 6.04% | 6.36% |
| *Dow-Jones* comp. avge. | 4.2 | 6.2 | 7.2 | 4.50 | 5.52 |
| *Dow-Jones* indl. avge. | 4.3 | 6.7 | 7.8 | 4.80 | 5.90 |

As can be seen, the higher return which was obtained on the averages during the first year was more than offset by the higher return on the growth stock portfolio in the past three years. From 1935 to 1938, the income on the supervised portfolio increased by 131%, while that on the stocks in the composite average was only 7% higher in 1938 than in 1935, and income on the industrial average increased 12%. In 1938 the income

9

on the growth stock portfolio was 34% higher than the income on the stocks in the composite average and 26% higher than that on the industrials alone.

### Maximum Gain with Minimum Risk

These figures of income and capital gain, which, it should be emphasized, are based on an *actual investment experience*, and not on a theoretical investment which might involve the use

CHART II
Growth Stock Portfolio Compared with Composite
Average, 1935-38

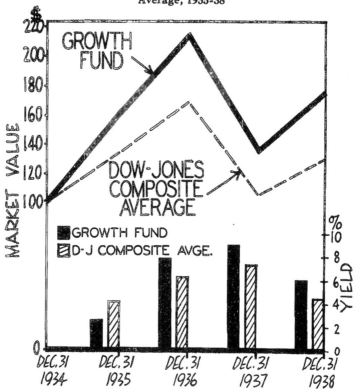

of hindsight, appear to furnish convincing evidence of the sound - ness of restricting holdings to corporations which are still in the earnings growth phase of their life cycle. Such a policy affords the maximum gain with the minimum risk. What is also important, the figures prove *it can be done*.

## Chapter II

# Measuring Industrial Life Cycles -
# The Fallacy of Investing for High Current Income

THE two best ways of measuring the life cycle of an industry are unit volume of sales and net earnings available for stockholders. It is important to consider both, for common stock investments should be confined to industries which are growing in both volume and earnings.

An excellent illustration of decadency in volume is afforded by the railroad industry. From 1902 to 1918 the average annual increase in ton miles of Class I railroads was 9.3%. During the after-war period from 1918 to 1926, average annual increase was only 1.3%. From 1926, the year railroads reached their peak volume, to 1929, business activity showed a further increase, but railroad ton miles declined 1.6%, indicating that the rail-

**CHART I**
**Railroads vs. Electric Power and Light Volume**
**1926=100**

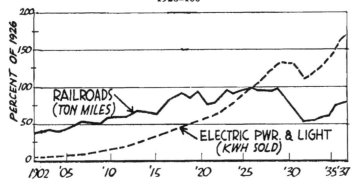

road industry had reached its maximum growth. The decline was greatly accentuated during the following depression years, and although there has been some recovery from the lows, ton miles in 1937 were still 19.7% under 1929 levels, thus definitely establishing a decadent long-term trend.

11

Compare, as does Chart I, the railroad life cycle with that of the power and light industry, which is still demonstrating healthy growth in volume. While the sale of kilowatt hours also declined in the depression following 1929, by the recovery year 1937 volume in this industry had risen 32% above the 1929 level. Though at a slower rate than in earlier years, the power and light industry is still growing in volume.

The trend of net earnings available for stockholders does not always tell the same story as volume of sales. The former, as in the case of the power and light industry, may have reached maturity while unit volume is still continuing to grow. In spite of an increase of 33% in kwh. from 1930 (the year of maximum earnings) to 1937, net earnings declined 24%. The power and light industry is still experiencing a strong growth in volume, but due to governmental control, competition and taxation, the long-term growth in earnings has probably reached maturity and may have entered the decadent phase of the industry life cycle, as measured in earnings.

When unit volume of an industry enters the decadent phase net earnings are likely to decline at a much faster rate than unit volume, as illustrated by the railroad industry. From 1929 (year of maximum earnings) to 1937, ton miles declined 19.7%, while net earnings declined 89%. The railroad industry obviously is decadent in both volume and earnings.

Effect of this circumstance on the prices of railroad stocks since 1926 is apparent, especially when they are compared with the progress of industrial stock prices. Chart II shows the greater gain possibilities and the smaller risk of loss afforded by industrial stocks as compared with rails. The year 1926 is used because it marked the end of growth in volume of the railroad industry. Mean prices (that is, the average of the high and low) are used instead of highs and lows because few people buy or sell at the tops or bottoms.

The risk of loss to the investor in railroad stocks, as measured by the *Dow-Jones* average, was 76.5%, compared with 14.8% for industrial stocks, or more than five times as great. The investor's opportunity to gain in a rising market was much greater in industrial stocks, which advanced 98% from the mean prices of 1932 to those of 1938. During the same period railroad stocks declined 3%. Even during the most favorable period for comparing railroad stocks with industrial stocks (1932-36) the opportunity for gain was 152% for industrials, compared with 84% for railroads.

### CHART II
Industrial vs. Railroad Stock Prices Based on Average Prices for Year
1926=100

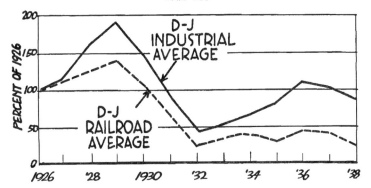

Within the industrial division of common stocks, there are, of course, variations in rate of growth. Many enterprises have long since reached maturity and are definitely decadent. Increased competition, new products, new inventions, new markets, consumers' preferences and many other factors are preventing many well-known corporations, popular among investors, from continuing their former spectacular growth and profits.

The chemical industry is one which is still experiencing a strong growth in earnings. In Chart III is illustrated the favorable growth of this industry compared with 932 industrial corporations which include many of the blue chips of former years. The middle line on the chart, which is the total of 19 chemical companies, represents the whole industry. The top line is the total of four companies which the author considers growth stocks.

"Growth stocks" can be defined as shares in business enterprises which have demonstrated favorable underlying long-term growth in earnings and which, after careful research study, give indications of continued secular growth in the future.

13

Secular, or underlying long-term growth, should not be confused with the cyclical recovery in earnings which takes place as business activity increases from a period of depression to a period of prosperity. Secular growth extends through several business cycles, with earnings reaching new high levels at the peak of each subsequent major business cycle.

Monsanto Chemical, for example, is classified as a growth stock because its 1929 (boom year) earnings of $2 a share were exceeded in the recovery year 1937, when the company earned $4.40 a share, and it is believed that during the next period of prosperity earnings a share will exceed those of 1937.

The fact that a stock is considered to be a growth stock is no assurance against a decline in income or market value during

CHART III
Earnings Available for Common Stock, Percent. Change since 1929

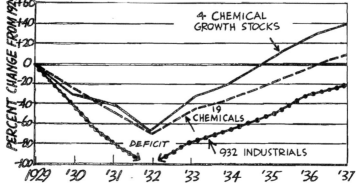

the downtrend of a business cycle, as growth stocks often depreciate as much as other groups. However, the prospects for recovery are more favorable for growth stocks than for matured and decadent stocks.

There are two major types of growth stocks—"cyclical growth" stocks and "stable growth" stocks. During periods of depression the earnings and dividends of most companies decline to a greater or lesser degree. The ones which fluctuate most widely with the ups and downs of the business cycles, like Chrysler, have been classified as "cyclical growth" stocks. The ones which have demonstrated relatively stable earnings and dividends during business depressions, like International Business Machines, have been classified as "stable growth" stocks.

Each of these two groups has different characteristics and qualifies for different investment purposes. A stable growth stock is more suitable for the investor requiring relatively stable income, while a cyclical growth stock is more suitable for the investor whose major objective is capital gain during a period of cyclical recovery.

In comparisons of changes in earnings, dividends and market value of growth, matured and decadent stocks, (See Chart IV, page 16), only stable growth stocks are included, because the matured and decadent groups are composed of relatively stable earners. Cyclical growth stocks will be included in a later list. The selection of stable growth stocks does not represent hindsight, so far as the period since 1934 is concerned, as all have been classified by the author as stable growth stocks during the past three to five years. The earlier part of the period does represent hindsight. The point of the comparisons, however, is to demonstrate the advantages, in long-term investing, of buying growth stocks. The list of stable growth stocks is contained in Table I. Of course, no such list is permanent. For

---

### TABLE I—STABLE GROWTH STOCKS, 1938*

| | | |
|---|---|---|
| Air Reduction | du Pont | J C Penney |
| Best | Humble Oil | Procter & Gamble |
| Coca-Cola | Int Bus Mach | Sherwin-Williams |
| Comm Inv Trust | Monsanto Chem | Union Carbide & C |
| Dow Chemical | Owens-Ill Glass | |

---

instance, factors now at work in the finance field may cause removal of Commercial Investment Trust, and other removals or additions to the list might become advisable.

"Matured stocks" are shares in business enterprises which, after careful study, appear to have reached their maximum earnings. The five stocks selected for this group represent

*Abbott Laboratories, Amerada, Dr. Pepper, Minnesota Min. & Mfg. and Scott Paper, recently added to Stable Growth Stock List, were excluded from calculations.

popular companies among investors today—American Can, American Tobacco, American Telephone, Continental Can and Reynolds Tobacco. The can and tobacco stocks were in the stable growth list until several years ago and there may be some question of the justification for now placing them in the matured group. There is no clear-cut line of demarcation and the change

**CHART IV**

**Percent. Change from 1929 of Growth, Matured and Decadent Stock Groups**

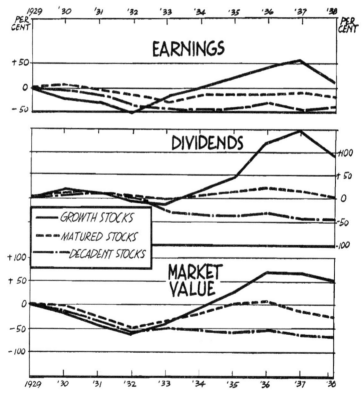

in trend is a matter of personal judgment until a definitely decadent trend of long-term earnings has been established. It is perfectly possible that one or more of these companies may report new high earnings a share at some future date.

"Decadent stocks" are defined as shares in business enterprises which are experiencing a long-term, or secular, decline in earnings. Five leading food stocks have been selected—Borden, General Foods[1], National Biscuit, National Dairy Products and Standard Brands—which showed impressive growth in earning power during the 1920's, but which have subsequently experienced a decline as a result of social, political and economic developments. In all probability, unless important new developments reverse the trend, they will be unable to register new high earnings a share in the future, although it is reasonable to expect some cyclical recovery from the low earnings of the past several years.

Chart IV shows the percentage changes in earnings, dividends and mean market prices of the three groups, by years, from 1929 through 1938. Comparing the peak recovery year, 1937, with the boom year, 1929, we find the results were as follows:

|  | Earnings | Dividends | Market value |
|---|---|---|---|
| Growth stocks | inc. 47.3% | inc. 148.4% | inc. 67.1% |
| Matured stocks | dec. 16.6% | inc. 18.3% | dec. 13.8% |
| Decadent stocks | dec. 56.5% | dec. 43.0% | dec. 61.0% |

There are two sound reasons for investing in common stocks —growth of income and growth of principal. Many investors prefer common stocks from which a high current income can be obtained. This is a fallacious policy because in the majority of cases a common stock which affords a relatively high yield at the time of purchase possesses a greater risk of reduction of income and loss in market value in the future.

This point is illustrated in Chart V (page 18). This chart is divided into two parts. The first part, 1929 through 1934, represents hindsight; the second part, 1934 through 1938, represents foresight, as it covers the period of practical application of the Life Cycle Theory.

Average income for the ten year period, 1929-1938, was 4.5% on the matured group, 4.2% on the growth stocks and

---

[1]General Foods has been mentioned in *Barron's* as a potential growth stock because of its Birdseye process, which is becoming increasingly popular. However, under Mr. Price's methods, the results of General Foods in recent years definitely class it as a "decadent" stock up to this point.

3.2% on the decadent stocks. The higher income on the matured stock group, taking the ten years as a whole, was the result of the fact that four of the stocks in the group continued to grow after 1929 and only reached maturity during the latter part of the decade under review. The growth stocks would compare more favorably if the comparison were limited to the past five years.

While stocks with matured and decadent earnings trends may yield more than growth stocks when purchased, over a period of several years growth stocks increase their dividends and, in the course of time, pay a better return on invested principal.

When the capital gain in the growth stocks is compared with the capital losses in the matured and decadent stocks, the results are even more convincing. One dollar invested in growth stocks in 1929 was worth, in 1938, twice as much as a dollar

CHART V
Yield on Investment Made at 1929 Mean Prices

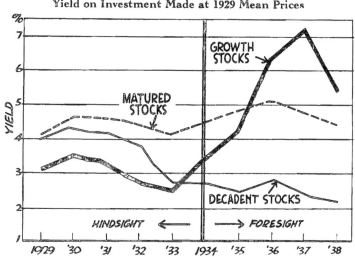

invested in matured stocks and five times as much as one dollar invested in decadent stocks.

Higher current income, it is evident, is obtained at the sacrifice of future income and the risk of loss of principal.

Chapter III

# Procedure of Selection Applied in Three Fields - Factors to Consider

NO mathematical formula or yardstick alone can be relied on for identifying growth stocks or for detecting when their earnings reach maturity. The requirements for an active, up-to-date list are arbitrary and should be revised periodically with each new business cycle as factual information and prudent judgment dictate.

The one requirement that does not change is that future earnings during periods of prosperity must give indications of exceeding previous peak earnings. Obviously, it would be impossible for anyone during times of depression to select 50 or more stocks and have all of them qualify as growth stocks during the following years. If the selection is 75% correct, however, investment results will be astonishingly good.

## Picking Out Most Attractive Industries

The selection of growth stocks necessitates careful analysis of past trends and sound judgment in appraising social, political and economic influences on business enterprises in the future. For example, if the long-term trend is away from private capitalism and toward State capitalism, such industries as communications, railroads, and power and light, which are likely to be controlled or dominated more and more by the Government, should be avoided.

The most fertile fields for the selection of growth stocks are:

1—New industries.

2—Divisions of old industries which are experiencing a vigorous growth as a result of new products, or new uses for old products.

3—Specialties which are expanding their products and markets.

## Why Certain Industries Forge Ahead

The first field includes such industries as air conditioning, aviation, Diesel engines, plastics and television. The second field includes alloy metals, business and office equipment, chemicals, electrical equipment and appliances, and machinery. Such companies as Coca-Cola Co., Minnesota Mining & Manufacturing, Scott Paper and Technicolor are included in the third field.

A study of the various companies within a new industry will reveal that certain ones are making greater progress than others. This may be the result of superior management, extensive research, valuable patents, influential sponsors, strong financial condition, favorable location, and many other factors. If, on further investigation, it is believed that such favorable factors may be expected to continue during the coming years, these may be selected as growth stocks.

## Favorable Prospect for Aviation

For example, aviation was still a relatively new industry in 1933, when an analysis led to the conclusion that certain divisions of the industry were in a good position to experience substantial growth. The favorable outlook for the transportation of passengers, mail and express by air and the obsolete equipment in use indicated a favorable trend in the demand for commercial airplanes. The United States Government's military airplanes were largely obsolete and far below the authorized numerical strength, and there was evidence that an effort would be made to correct the situation. The trend toward rearmament throughout the world had started, and the growing recognition of the superiority of American-made commercial and military equipment gave the export market a promising outlook.

In addition to the promise of growth in volume of commercial and military equipment sales, it seemed probable that profit margins would improve, enabling earnings to grow at a faster rate than volume. Engineering, development and production costs are very high in the industry, and the difficulty of absorbing these costs would decrease as volume of sales expanded. Because the growth of individual companies was less certain than the growth of the industry as a whole, it was considered more essential to diversify the risk over a number of companies than in the case of a seasoned industry.

On Dec. 15, 1933, a group of five stocks was selected to participate in the growth of the aviation industry. The reasons for the choice were the following:

1—They were leaders in the production of military and commercial engines, planes, propellers and instruments.

2—They were financially strong enough to withstand several years of adversity.

3—They enjoyed strong sponsorship.

4—They held valuable patents.

5—They had the benefit of experienced engineering and research staffs.

The following table lists the five stocks and shows the percentage gain in market value between Dec. 15, 1933, when the selection was made, and the end of 1938.

| Common shares | | Mkt. value 12/15/33 | Mkt. value 12/31/38 | % Gain |
|---|---|---|---|---|
| 50 | Curtiss-Wright | $125.00 | †$378.00 | 202% |
| 10 | Douglas Aircraft | 143.75 | †840.00 | 485 |
| 20 | North American Aviation | 102.50 | 398.00 | 288 |
| 20 | Sperry Corporation | 130.00 | 960.00 | 638 |
| 5 | United Aircraft & Trans | 165.63 | †*304.00 | 84 |
| | | 666.88 | 2,880.00 | 332% |

*Includes securities distributed in the reorganization. †Includes average value of rights.

While the market value of this group of stocks had increased 332% as of Dec. 31, 1938, there were wide variations in individual results. At the time of selection, United Aircraft & Transport was regarded as the soundest company, and yet it showed the least appreciation. Sperry Corp. had the greatest appreciation, although at the time of selection its growth possibilities were less apparent than those of some of the other units.

Many investors have avoided aviation stocks because of the excessive risk involved, preferring to purchase stocks of established industries with far less opportunity for growth, such as the railroads and automobiles.

## Aircraft versus Automobiles

The recent growth of the aviation industry and that of the well-established automobile industry are compared in Chart I. During the recovery years 1936 and 1937 automobile production failed to equal 1929 levels, while airplane production, measured

**CHART I**
Airplane vs. Automobile Production
(1929=100)

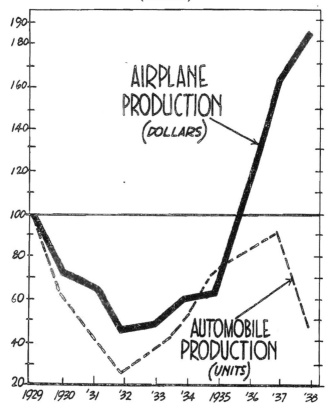

in dollars, reached a new high level. By 1938 airplane production was 84.4% higher than in 1929, while automobile production had declined 53.5%. Although it is true that aviation has been greatly stimulated by war preparations, commercial use of the airplane is growing at a rapid rate, as measured by the increase in passenger, mail and express transportation. Such commercial business, however, is quite small in relation to military volume and could not be counted on for uninterrupted growth in total aircraft volume in the unlikely event of a sudden cessation of military business.

While there were periods during the interim when holders of aviation stocks had just reason to be concerned, the actual risk of holding equities of a decadent industry, like railroads, proved to be much greater, as the following comparison shows:

|  | % Change<br>12/15/33–12/31/38 |
|---|---|
| *Dow-Jones* Railroad Average | − 19 |
| *Dow-Jones* Industrial Average | + 53 |
| Selected aviation stocks | +332 |

### Vigorous Growth in Old Industries

The metal industry is well established and represents one of the major fields for investment. While the better known metals, such as iron, lead, zinc, copper and tin have been used in great quantities for a long time, the growth in the use of aluminum and nickel has been most pronounced during recent years.

All of the qualifications of a growth stock in an old industry are possessed by the International Nickel Co., which produces over 85% of the world's output of nickel. Its management is capable and progressive; its products enjoy a wide market; its financial condition is sound; its earnings record is well established over several business cycles and its stock is a seasoned investment with a world market.

A number of years ago it seemed that a further investigation of the alloying metals might reveal a new opportunity for the investor seeking growth stocks, because the trend during recent years, particularly in the transportation industry, had been toward speed, thus necessitating the increased use of metals for lighter and stronger alloy steels. Study led to the selection of molybdenum as a metal that should experience new uses. Small quantities of this alloying element act to increase the elastic limit, hardness, impact and fatigue values of steel, and enhance the corrosion resisting abilities of stainless steels.

Climax Molybdenum Co. was found to be the most important company in the field, owning the largest molybdenum mine in

23

the world and producing approximately 75% of the world's output. The stock, therefore, was selected in the early part of 1935 as a highly speculative issue which possessed a greater growth factor than International Nickel because of its relatively small use and large potential market. At the same time, it involved a much greater risk to the investor, due to the possible discovery and development of new deposits by other companies

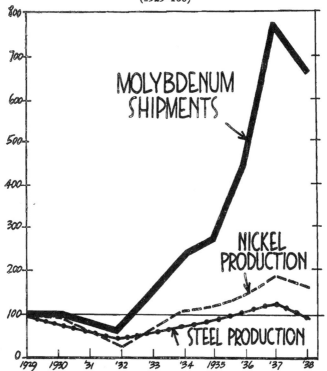

CHART II
Progress in the Metal Industry
(1929=100)

with stronger financial resources, competition from other alloys with resultant loss of market for its products, and potential operating difficulties during the developmental stages.

Since the alloying metals, nickel and molybdenum, are used largely in the manufacture of steel, a comparison of nickel production and molybdenum shipments, and the world production of steel ingots and castings for the past 10 years illustrates their relative growth. This is shown in Chart II.

The years 1929 and 1937 represent the peaks of world steel production during the past two business cycles. Molybdenum shipments grew 671% between these dates, while nickel production increased 85% and steel production gained only 12%. Comparing the depression years 1934 and 1938, the relative growth of the two alloying metals is again demonstrated: Molybdenum shipments were 174% higher in 1938 than in 1934, nickel production was up 63% and steel production gained 31%. A large proportion of Molybdenum shipments, however, is represented by export business and is probably for armaments, suggesting dependence of the company on continuance of the armament race, which at present seems probable.

While International Nickel Co. and Climax Molybdenum are both growth stocks, the latter has grown at the faster rate, as the following figures illustrate:

|  | Climax Molybdenum | | International Nickel | |
|---|---|---|---|---|
|  | Earnings | Divs. | Earnings | Divs. |
| 1938 | $3.12 | $2.20 | $2.09 | $2.00 |
| 1937 | 2.85 | 1.70 | 3.32 | 2.25 |
| 1936 | 2.07 | 1.00 | 2.39 | 1.30 |
| 1935 | 1.28 | .69 | 1.66 | .75 |
| 1934 | .71 | .07 | 1.14 | .50 |
| % gain, 1934-38 | 340% | | 83% | |

The earnings and dividends a share of Climax Molybdenum exceeded those of International Nickel for the first time in 1938. In the same year Climax reached a new high and, also for the first time, the stock sold at a higher price than International Nickel.

### Growing Specialty Companies

Scott Paper Company is an illustration of a specialty company which has expanded its products and developed its markets. Its growth should continue because of the following factors:

1—The potential market in this country for paper towels is only partially developed.

2—Aggressive sales and advertising methods should enable it to gain a larger share of the existing market for paper products.

3—Potential addition of allied paper products.

4—The possibility of expanding foreign markets.

5—Ability to maintain satisfactory margin of profit with rapidly increasing sales.  (See Chart III).

The cases discussed in this chapter illustrate some of the most important factors considered in the identification of growth stocks.  Others, such as (1) trend in rate of return on invested

CHART III
Growth of Scott Paper Co.
1925–38

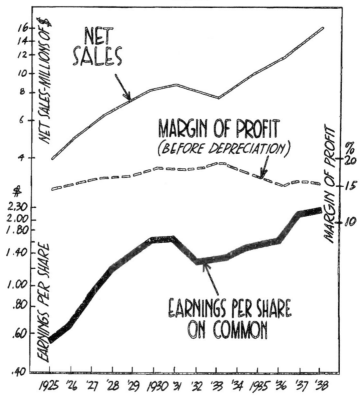

capital; (2) relationship and trend of labor costs to net earnings; (3) relationship and trend of taxes to net earnings; (4) legislation; (5) inventions; (6) expiration of patents; (7) competition; (8) change in management, are discussed in the next chapter.

## Chapter IV

# *How to Detect the Change from Growth to Maturity - Chrysler vs. General Motors*

DETECTING with a high degree of accuracy when the long-term earnings growth of a company has ceased is difficult because no mathematical formula can be applied to determine when the change from growth to maturity or decadence occurs. There is no clear line of demarcation between the three phases because (1) the business cycle and a company's life cycle, which usually extends over several business cycles, run concurrently, and (2) those factors which adversely affect a company's secular earnings growth often assert themselves during a period of depression when earnings are low.

A cyclical decline in earnings due to a general business depression may be wrongly interpreted as the end of secular growth. Likewise, a cyclical recovery in earnings may be mistaken for a continuation or resumption of secular growth.

Aside from the general business cycle which affects almost all businesses, some industries, such as real estate and oil, have their own cycles of prosperity and decline. The real estate cycle usually requires about 18 years for completion, while the oil industry is influenced by the discovery of new flush fields which cause overproduction and depressed prices for oil and gasoline.

In attempting to determine the position of a particular company in its period of growth or decline, not only must the business cycle and the cycle of that company's industry be considered but also many factors which may affect the secular trend of the company in varying degrees must be taken into account. Not all the companies of a certain industry may be affected by the same factors and certainly not all to the same extent. Sound judgment is required to appraise the relative importance of these other influences on each individual company.

## 10 Considerations

Some of the most important factors are:

1. Change in management.
2. Saturation of markets.
3. New inventions.
4. Expiration of patents.
5. Increased competition.
6. Adverse legislation.
7. Unfavorable court decisions.
8. Sharp rise in the cost of materials.
9. Sharp rise in labor costs.
10. Increase in taxes.

In some instances one factor, such as adverse legislation or expiration of patents, may be wholly responsible for changes in secular earnings trends; in other instances a combination of factors may be the cause. The results can be measured by a study of the trends in (1) sales, (2) profit margin and (3) return on invested capital.

### Interrupted Growth in the Utilities Industry

The power and light industry is an excellent illustration of how numerous adverse factors occurring during a depression can check the secular earnings growth of companies whose common stocks appeared to qualify as growth stocks prior to the depression. Companies in this industry possessed a strong secular earnings growth in 1929, and for many months after the depression started net earnings continued to increase, reaching new high levels in 1930 and showing only a slight decline in 1931.

Up until the advent of the New Deal in 1933, which was after the lows of the depression had been reached, it was a reasonable expectation that earnings of the power and light industry would recover to new high levels during a subsequent period of prosperity because of the favorable outlook for growth in electric power production. However, government competition, persistent and successful efforts to lower rates and a sharp rise in taxes reduced the industry's profit margin.

It was not until January, 1938, that further developments, including (1) an adverse decision by the Supreme Court; (2) the failure of the Government to compromise in the fight with the utility industry; and (3) a new business recession accompanied by an increase in inflationary measures, led to the decision to

28

remove the power and light stocks from the growth list. It will probably be several years before it can be established whether or not the end of secular growth in earnings has occurred.

## A Contrast in Two Companies

While most of the companies in this industry have failed so far to recover to their former high earnings, the Pennsylvania

CHART I

Two Utility Companies Compare

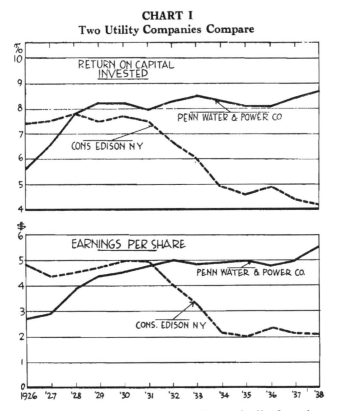

Water & Power Co. has been an exception and affords an interesting comparison with Consolidated Edison Co. of New York, which has been subjected to a number of adverse factors referred to above. Earnings a share and the return on invested capital of these two companies since 1926 are shown in Chart I.

There were a number of factors in the spring of 1933 that

indicated a change in the secular growth in the earnings of Consolidated Edison. With the advent of the New Deal and its antagonism toward the power and light interests, this company was believed to be in a very vulnerable position. Its management was not progressive in its public relations, electric and gas rates were high, depreciation charges were low, and higher costs of material and labor and higher taxes seemed inevitable. While steps have been taken during subsequent years to correct some of these adverse factors, the 7.7% return on invested capital for the year 1930 has declined to 4.2% in 1938, and it is doubtful whether the company will be able to exceed previous peak earnings in the discernible future in view of the difficulty of increasing its rates sufficiently to offset the probable further rise in costs and taxes.

The high return on invested capital, which has enabled the Pennsylvania Water & Power Co. to make such a creditable showing, may prove to be unfavorable for the company in the years ahead, as a recent Supreme Court decision makes it vulnerable to a reduction in rates, which would result in a decline in earnings a share.

## Advent of Competition

Continental Can Co. illustrates how adverse legislation and increased competition can check the earnings growth of a well-managed company in an industry which is still growing in volume

### TABLE I
#### Continental Can Co., 1934-38

|  | Invested capital | Net sales* | Profit margin before deprec. | Earns a share |
|---|---|---|---|---|
| 1938 | $118,015,024 | $85,673,999 | 12.8% | $2.17 |
| 1937 | 117,480.540 | 93,879,021 | 13.6 | 3.06 |
| 1936 | 97,865,405 | 91,172,066 | 14.3 | 3.17 |
| 1935 | 89,000,399 | 80,923,392 | 19.6 | 4.21 |
| 1934 | 84.029,350 | 68,207,135 | 22.7 | 4.02 |
| % change 1934-38 | +40% | +26% | −44.0% | −46% |

*Net sales to outside customers.

of sales. This stock was classified as a growth stock until the middle of 1936, when it became apparent that the passage of the Robinson-Patman Act and the entry of Crown Cork & Seal and

Owens-Illinois Glass companies into the tin can business would likely reduce the profit margins and possibly prevent the company from continuing its favorable secular earnings growth.

During the five years, 1925 to 1929, inclusive, Continental Can's earnings averaged $2.91 a share and dividends averaged $1.67 a share. The next five years, 1930 to 1934, inclusive, notwithstanding the depression, were almost as good, earnings having averaged $2.86 and dividends $1.65 a share. By 1934 earnings of $4.02 exceeded the previous high earnings in 1925 of $3.59, thus confirming the belief that Continental Can was still a growth company.

Although general business continued to improve during 1936 and 1937, earnings for the above company declined, as shown in Table I, indicating that the secular growth had ceased. The figures in the table measure the results of adverse legislation and competition. Although invested capital increased 40%, sales were only 26% higher, while profit margin declined 44% and earnings a share 46%.

While it is possible that at some time in the future this company may be able to overcome the adverse factors which interrupted secular growth, the uncertainties appear sufficient to disqualify it as a growth stock, at least for the present.

### Chrysler vs. General Motors

A comparison of Chrysler Corp. with General Motors Corp. illustrates the importance, when trying to detect the end of secular earnings growth, of measuring both growth in the volume of sales and the trend in return on invested capital. While the trend in profit margins is one of the most important factors considered, it is not always the company which reports the higher profit margin that proves to be the better growth stock. Sometimes a company which has a relatively low profit margin is able greatly to increase its sales volume without increasing its capital investment and thereby increase its earnings per share.

The growth of the automobile industry appeared to be reaching maturity in the late 'twenties, yet two of the leading companies continued to grow by increasing their share of the total production of the industry, as shown in Table II (page 32).

31

In 1934 both General Motors and Chrysler were on the growth stock list as it was believed that both companies would be able to report new high earnings a share during the recovery period.

The trend in sales, profit margins and return on invested capital for the two companies are compared in Chart II and Chart III. Chrysler's dollar sales were growing at a faster rate than General Motors', amounting to $517,000,000 in 1935, and exceeding the previous high level of $375,000,000 reported in 1929. By 1936 sales had reached $667,000,000, an increase over 1929 of 78%. The profit margin of 11% in 1936 compared favorably with 10.8% in 1928. Earnings a share reached a new high level of $14.25,

### TABLE II
Share of General Motors and Chrysler in Total Production of Automobile Industry

PERCENT. OF TOTAL AUTOMOBILE PRODUCTION IN U. S.

|  | Chrysler | Gen. Motors | Chrysler and Gen. Motors combined |
|---|---|---|---|
| 1938 | 21.5% | 41.7% | 63.2% |
| 1937 | 23.1 | 38.4 | 61.5 |
| 1936 | 23.1 | 40.4 | 63.5 |
| 1935 | 20.5 | 38.0 | 58.5 |
| 1934 | 20.8 | 39.3 | 60.1 |
| 1933 | 22.7 | 40.4 | 63.1 |
| 1932 | 15.6 | 36.7 | 52.3 |
| 1931 | 11.0 | 41.8 | 52.8 |
| 1930 | 7.7 | 33.0 | 40.7 |
| 1929 | 8.0 | 33.8 | 41.8 |
| 1928 | 7.8 | 39.3 | 47.1 |
| 1927 | 5.4 | 43.6 | 49.0 |
| 1926 | 3.8 | 27.4 | 31.2 |
| 1925 | 3.1 | 18.9 | 22.0 |

as compared with the predepression peak of $6.80 a share, thus confirming the belief that Chrysler was still a growth stock.

### Motors Had Higher Profit Margin

General Motors Corp. dollar sales of $1,439,000,000 in 1936 likewise recovered sharply from the depression, but were 4.4% lower than in 1929. While the company's profit margin of 19.7% in 1936 was slightly lower than the 21.1% reported in 1928, it was materially higher than the 11% for Chrysler. Earnings of $5.35 a share in 1936 failed to reach the previous high level of $6.05 a share reported in 1928.

During the period 1928 to 1936 General Motors retained part of its earnings in the business, thus increasing invested capital by approximately 22%, while Chrysler reduced its invested capital by 20%. The charts show that while the General

**CHART II**
**Chrysler and General Motors Compared**

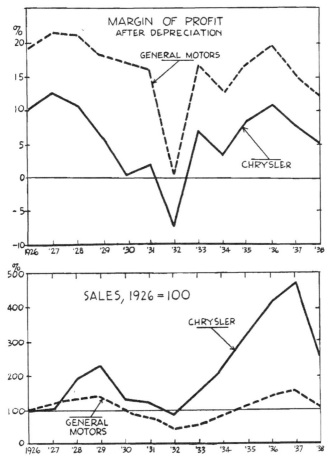

Motors profit margin was higher than Chrysler's and fairly well maintained, the return on invested capital declined 27% from 1928 to 1936, while the return on Chrysler's invested capital increased 53%. Earnings a share in the case of General Motors

declined 11.6%; earnings a share in the case of Chrysler increased 110%.

As recovery progressed, it appeared that the General Motors earnings growth was fast reaching maturity. In January, 1937,

### CHART III
#### Chrysler and General Motors Compared

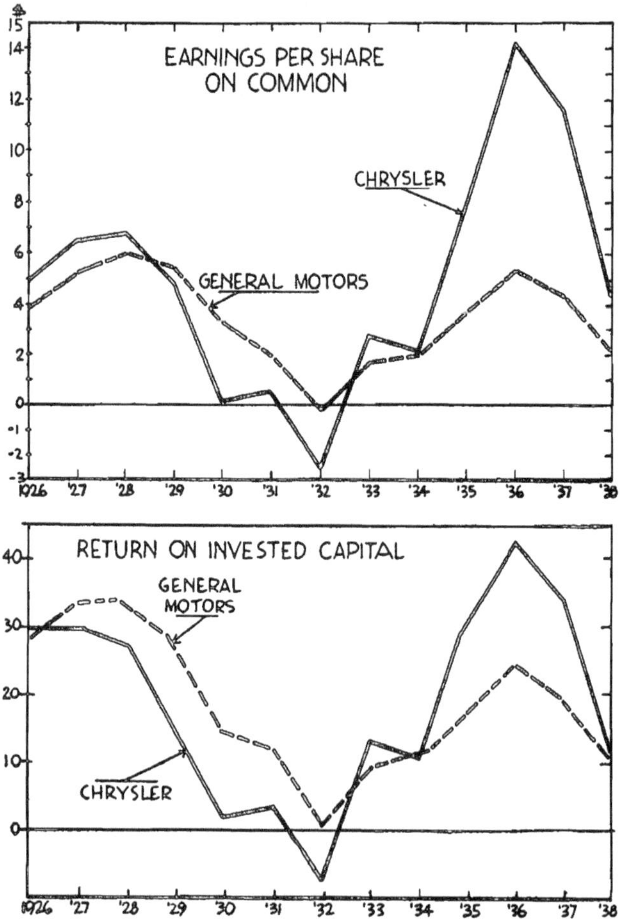

it became evident that General Motors labor would be unionized, with a resulting increase in labor costs. Because the growth in earnings appeared to be reaching maturity prior to that event, it was concluded that higher labor costs would prevent General Motors from qualifying as a growth stock and it was, therefore, removed from the list.

**CHART IV**
Mathieson Alkali Works, Inc.

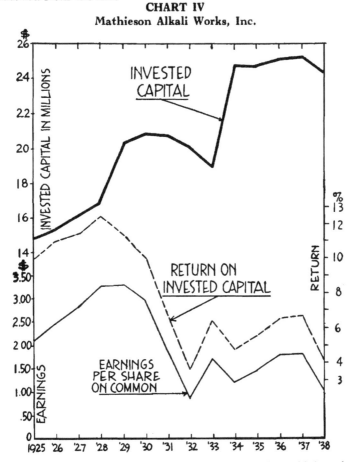

Chrysler was also handicapped by unionization of labor, but because it still possessed more favorable prospects for growth in sales volume, it was retained on the list of growth stocks.

If increasing capital investment does not increase the profits, a decline in the return on invested capital results. This declining trend is a warning signal.

The chart on Mathieson Alkali Works, Inc., (Chart IV) is presented as an illustration of the importance of detecting diminishing return on invested capital. The company produces basic chemicals, such as soda ash, caustic soda, chlorine and allied products, and serves consumers goods industries. Since Mathieson does not make a practice of publishing its dollar sales, it has been impossible to study the trend in profit margins.

Earnings experienced a substantial growth during the 1920's and the return on invested capital was at a satisfactory level. Although earnings and the return on invested capital declined during the following depression, early in 1934 the stock of this company was considered for the growth stock list due to the possibility that the earnings growth would be resumed and the return on invested capital would recover.

However, the company had just increased its capital stock $33\frac{1}{3}\%$ to provide funds for the construction of a large plant in Louisiana. Two competitors were likewise constructing plants in the South. A study of the capacity of the industry indicated that the additional capacity was not necessary, and Mathieson was believed to have invested this additional capital as a defensive measure to protect its markets in an area where it had previously enjoyed a freight advantage.

Under the circumstances, an improved return on invested capital and earnings per share were not expected and the stock was not included in the list. The average return on invested capital in recent years has been under 6% and is not commensurate with the risk involved in placing equity money in a company which seems to have reached maturity.

The above cases are cited from actual experience and are intended to help the investor detect changes in secular earnings trends in time to withdraw his funds from an investment before the decadent earnings trend becomes so obvious that the market has discounted the changed value. The causes of the change can often be detected before the results can be measured in terms of sales, profit margins and return on invested capital.

The following list of stocks includes all the stocks which were held as probable growth stocks during the five year period 1934-1939. They have been divided into three groups: (1) Those which have already proved to be growth stocks because

36

subsequent earnings per share have exceeded previous maximum earnings per share; (2) Those stocks which are expected to reach new high earnings at a later time when it is anticipated that business for the respective industries will be more profitable; (3) Those stocks which have been withdrawn because subsequent events have indicated that maximum earnings have already been reached.

# GROWTH STOCKS

## Group I

Those which have already proved to be Growth stocks because subsequent earnings a share have exceeded previous maximum earnings a share

Abbott Laboratories
Addressograph- Multigraph
Air Reduction
Allis-Chalmers
Best & Co.
Borg Warner
Briggs
Carrier Corp.
Chrysler
Climax Molybdenum
Coca-Cola
Comm'l Credit
Comm'l Invest. Tr.
Curtiss-Wright
Douglas Aircraft
Dow Chemical
Dr. Pepper
du Pont
Eastern Air Lines
Fidelity & Deposit
Humble Oil
Int'l Business Machines

Int'l Nickel
Libbey-Owens-Ford
Martin, Glenn L.
Masonite
Minn.-Honeywell Reg.
Minnesota Min. & Mfg.
Monsanto Chemical
National Gypsum
No. Am. Aviation
Owens-Illinois Glass
J. C. Penney
Procter & Gamble
Royal Typewriter
Scott Paper
Servel
Sherwin Williams
Sperry Corp.
Square D
Standard Oil of N. J.
Union Carbide
United Aircraft

## Group II

Those stocks which are expected to reach new high earnings at a later time when it is anticipated that business for the respective industries will be more profitable

Amerada
Am. Smelt. & Refg.
Black & Decker
Continental Oil
Crane
Gen'l Am. Transp.
General Electric
Gulf Oil

Holland Furnace
Johns-Manville
Kennecott Copper
Montgomery Ward
Phelps Dodge
Phillips Petroleum
Remington Rand
Sears Roebuck

## Group II (continued)

| | |
|---|---|
| Standard Oil of California | United Air Lines |
| Technicolor | U. S. Fidelity & Guaranty |
| Texas Pacific Land Trust | U. S. Gypsum |
| Timken Roller Bearing | Westinghouse Electric |

## Group III

Those stocks which have been withdrawn because subsequent events have indicated that maximum earnings may have already been reached

| | |
|---|---|
| American Can | General Motors |
| American Gas & Electric | International Harvester |
| American Tobacco | Liggett & Myers |
| Caterpillar Tractor | North American Co. |
| Commonwealth Edison | Pacific Gas & Electric |
| Cons. G. E. L. & Pw., Balt. | Pacific Lighting |
| Continental Can | Pennsy. Water & Power |
| Cutler Hammer | Public Service of N. J. |
| Deere & Co. | Reynolds Tobacco |
| Detroit Edison | United Gas Improvement |

The recovery period 1936-1937 was unbalanced and was not an adequate test for all industries. The building and construction industry, for example, recovered to less than 50% of its predepression level, and building companies as a group have not had an opportunity to develop their maximum earning power. General American Transportation Corp. in the railroad equipment industry appears to be a company which might well attain new high earnings when railroads materially increase their expenditures for equipment in order to handle increased freight during a period of prosperity for the construction industry. Electrical equipments represent a third group which should develop new high earnings when the power and light industry increases deferred expenditures for new generating facilities. Certain producing oils and coppers are retained as growth stocks because it is believed that inflation will enable these companies to report higher earnings a share than during the recent recovery period.

## Chapter V

# "Stable" and "Cyclical" Types
# Permit Flexibility in Portfolio Management

GROWTH stocks are as varied in their characteristics as a surgeon's instruments or a carpenter's tools and, similarly, successful results are dependent on knowledge and experience in their proper use. Some growth companies pay regular dividends; some irregular, while others distribute no dividends at all. Some pay out nearly all of their earnings; others pay a portion and reinvest the rest in the business in order to produce higher earnings and dividends for future distribution. Thus, from the standpoint of income, types vary greatly.

Growth stocks also differ greatly in quality. Some represent shares in well established companies, like General Electric Co. which is the leader in its field both as to size, diversification of products and financial strength. Others, such as Square D Co., may be largely dependent on a few products and are, therefore, more vulnerable to competition, new patents, etc., while still others, due to financial weakness, may be unable to withstand a prolonged depression.

## Two Groupings

For the sake of simplicity all growth stocks have been divided into two major groups—stable growth and cyclical growth. Recognizing that stocks vary greatly in quality, each of the major groups has been further divided into two quality groups—first grade and second grade. Generally speaking, smaller companies, those with a very limited number of products or largely dependent on a few patents, or unseasoned companies have been placed in the lower quality groups.

Stable growth stocks are shares in companies with relatively stable earnings and dividend payments,' while cyclical growth stocks are shares in companies with cyclical earnings and dividend

39

payments. Coca-Cola Co. (Chart I) is an example of the first type; International Nickel Co. of Canada, Ltd.(Chart II) is an example of the second type. Both attained new high earnings and dividends a share following the 1932 depression. However, in the case of Coca-Cola earnings were well maintained throughout the depression, and dividends, during the 1930-34 period

## EARNINGS AND DIVIDEND TRENDS

### CHART I

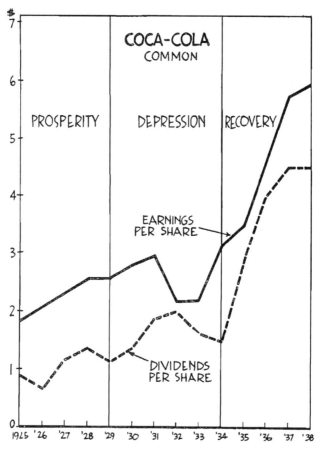

averaged 61% above the 1925-29 period of prosperity. In the case of International Nickel earnings disappeared temporarily during the worst of the depression, and for two years the stockholders received no dividends at all. Obviously, a stable growth stock like Coca-Cola was far more suitable for an endowment fund or a trust estate requiring regular income than was International Nickel.

**EARNINGS AND DIVIDEND TRENDS**
**CHART II**

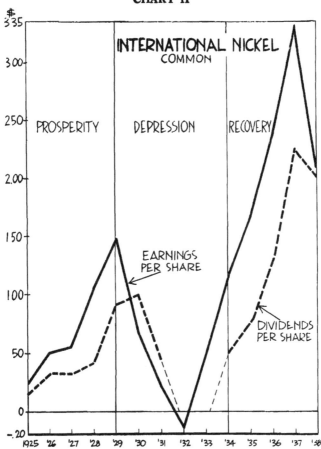

On the other hand, International Nickel offered greater opportunity for appreciation in market value than Coca-Cola if purchased during depression periods and, consequently, was better suited for the investor whose primary objective was capital growth at that time, as the following figures indicate:

|  | 1932 low | 1937 high | Advance |
|---|---|---|---|
| Coca-Cola | $17\frac{1}{8}$ | $170\frac{1}{2}$ | 896% |
| International Nickel | $3\frac{1}{2}$ | $73\frac{3}{8}$ | 1996 |
|  | 1938 low | 1938 high | Advance |
| Coca-Cola | $105\frac{1}{8}$ | $143\frac{3}{4}$ | 35% |
| International Nickel | $36\frac{7}{8}$ | $57\frac{7}{8}$ | 56 |

During 1935 and 1936, when the author's growth stock theory was first being applied to an actual fund, a procedure for dividing stocks into the two major groups—stable growth and cyclical growth—was developed. A study of each company's earnings and dividend record during the preceding decade under varying business conditions provided the best clue to what might be expected in the future under similar conditions. At that time, the following requirements were established for each of the groups, the requirements being based partially on past statistics and partially on judgment regarding the future.

## Requirements for Stable Growth Stocks

*Earnings:* Average earnings for the five depression years (1930-34, inclusive) must exceed 50% of the average earnings of the five prosperity years (1925-29, inclusive). The 1936 earnings must exceed 75% of the prosperity average. Indications must be that future earnings will continue favorable trend, with reasonable expectations that record high earnings will be attained before major recovery cycle is completed.

*Dividends:* Average dividends paid during the five depressions years (1930-34, inclusive) must exceed 50% of the average dividend paid during the five prosperity years (1925-29, inclusive). Dividends paid in 1936 must exceed 75% of the average for the five prosperity years, with estimated 1937 dividends indicating continuation of favorable trend.

## Requirements for Cyclical Growth Stocks

*FIRST GRADE:*

*Earnings:* Earnings for the five prosperity years (1925-29) must have shown a favorable trend. The 1936 earnings must

42

have given indications that new high earning power is likely before the major business recovery cycle has been completed.

*Dividends:* Stock must be on a dividend basis with favorable prospects for increase over the near term, reaching new high levels by the time the major business recovery cycle has been completed.

*SECOND GRADE:*

*Earnings:* Earnings record for a period of at least five years must be available, with indications that the secular trend is upward and will continue so.

*Dividends:* No dividend record is essential, but indications should be such that dividend payments are a reasonable expectation in the near future.

Naturally, when all stocks are divided into two general classifications, many border-line cases exist. For example, Air Reduction, du Pont and Union Carbide & Carbon might well be classified as cyclical growth stocks, although they met the above requirements of stable growth stocks. Periodic revisions of the mathematical formulae are necessary to keep abreast of the ever-changing economic and political trends.

Stable growth stocks are listed in the second chapter. Among all the stable growth stocks so classified here only Dr. Pepper and Minnesota Mining are regarded as of second grade at present, and this classification may be changed at any time. Cyclical growth stocks are not here subdivided according to quality, because changes in their rating are more frequent than in the case of stable growth stocks.

## The Dividend Angle

One of the major objectives of investors who buy common stocks is income. That such grouping as referred to above has a distinct value in portfolio management is illustrated by Chart III, which compares dividends paid on first grade stable growth stocks with dividends paid on first grade cyclical growth stocks.

Although the growth stock theory has been applied only since 1934, the chart (Chart III) was carried back to 1929 to show what happened during the great depression. The first part, 1929-34, represents hindsight; the second part, 1934-38, represents foresight. The dividends on the stable growth stocks declined a maximum of only 11.3% from 1929 to 1933, which was the

CHART III

Stable vs. Cyclical Growth Stocks

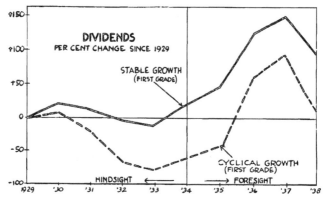

low year for dividends during the depression. With business recovery, dividends increased until they reached a maximum in 1937, when they were 148.4% higher than in 1929.

The dividends on the cyclical growth stocks declined a maximum of 78.3% from 1929 to 1933, then increased with recovery, reaching a new high in 1937, when they were 94.9% above the 1929 level. Both gains were somewhat exaggerated by the undistributed profits tax which forced numerous companies to pay higher dividends in the years 1936 and 1937.

Likewise, the decline of 22.7% in dividends on stable growth stocks from 1937 to 1938, and 44.8% on cyclical growth stocks for the same period, was exaggerated due to the revision of the undistributed profit tax law. Notwithstanding the temporary distortion on the upside, the investor in the stable group has enjoyed relatively stable income, as well as growth of income, as

44

compared to the investor in the cyclical group. The importance of selecting the right type of stock when regular income is of primary consideration is thus clearly demonstrated.

An index of dividends on second grade stable growth stocks is not plotted, since only two stocks are currently in this group and these have been added during recent months. Likewise, the dividend index on second grade cyclical growth stocks has not been plotted because this group consists largely of newer and unseasoned companies, many of which have not been placed on a regular dividend basis.

## Capital Appreciation Opportunities

Another major objective of investors who buy common stocks is growth of principal. Chart IV compares the market

### CHART IV
#### Market Action of Group Averages

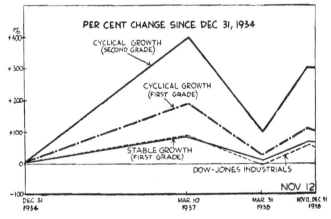

action of the first grade stable growth and first and second grade cyclical growth stocks. (Second grade stable growth stocks are excluded for reasons mentioned previously.) The four year period under consideration includes both business recovery and recession.

As would be expected, stable growth stocks showed the smallest rise from 1934 to the 1937 high, and the smallest decline from the 1937 high to the 1938 low. While stable growth stocks

45

rose 86% the first grade cyclical stocks advanced 186%. On the decline the former lost 42% and the latter 57%.

Second grade cyclical stocks, which are highly speculative, were outstanding on the upside, having advanced 399%, but likewise suffered the greatest decline, 61%. While the second grade cyclical index at the low point of 1938 was substantially above the others, a more serious depression might well have caused it to decline below both of the other indices. The degree of fluctuation usually varies with the degree of risk. The opportunity for greatest capital growth, therefore, is obtainable in the securities involving the greatest risk, but such securities rarely possess regular income characteristics.

If relatively stable income is important, a large portion of the common stock fund should be invested in stable growth stocks. If stable income is not important and emphasis is to be placed on growth in principal, a large portion of the fund should be invested in cyclical growth stocks, especially if stocks are purchased during periods of depression, as cyclical growth stocks afford the greatest profit possibilities. If stocks are purchased during prosperous times, when market values are high, stable growth stocks are the least hazardous. If large profits are desired and a high degree of risk can be assumed, and income is unimportant, then second grade cyclical growth stocks should qualify best.

The four-year record of the growth stock fund, referred to in these chapters, had as its major objective growth of income. Its program was especially designed to meet the requirements of trust funds, endowment funds and individual investors desiring regular income at an increasing rate to offset the decreasing return on bonds due to the Government's easy money policy. Only dividend-paying stocks qualified for this type of fund. The more highly speculative group, or second grade cyclical stocks with their greater capital gain possibilities, could not be used because of the uncertainty of dividends and the high risk factor involved.

### How Combined Investments Fared

A combination of growth of income and capital was attained by shifting the percentage invested in stable growth and cyclical growth stocks during various phases of the business cycle. For

46

illustration, in 1935 stable growth stocks represented only 34% of the total portfolio, while cyclical growth stocks, which were relatively low in market value, represented approximately 66%. As recovery progressed and stocks began to overdiscount future earnings, cyclical stocks sold relatively higher on an investment basis than stable stocks. The percentage invested in this type was, therefore, gradually reduced in the years 1937 and 1938 until it represented only 35% of the total fund.

More recently the trend has been reversed in anticipation of improved earnings for the cyclical stocks. Such a policy has proved advantageous, as the results indicate, and illustrates in actual practice another use of the various types of growth stocks in portfolio management. Knowing the characteristics of the various types of securities and using each judiciously in accordance with its potentialities should help the investor to achieve his desired objective with the minimum risk to capital.

Printed in the USA
CPSIA information can be obtained
at www.ICGtesting.com
LVHW021752080224
771343LV00002B/33